Nothing to it but to do it
A Common Sense Guide to Your Dream Job

Davy Z Jones

The author and publisher have made every effort to ensure that the information in this book was correct at the time of publication. The author and publisher do not assume and hereby disclaim any liability to any party for any loss, damage, or disruption caused by errors or omissions, whether such errors or omissions result from negligence, accident, or any other cause.

DISCLAIMERS – This publication was produced to provide general information about how to use common sense to search for a dream job. Information presented herein is intended to be used for general educational purposes only and should not be construed to be offered in any way as career counseling or to guarantee success in any job search.

NO LEGAL ADVICE OFFERED -- Content herein is not intended to convey or constitute legal advice, is not intended to be a solicitation of any kind, and is in no way is a substitution for advice obtained from a qualified career counselor. We advise you to consult with the career counselor of your choice for answers to your questions.

USE OF THIS PUBLICATION -- This publication is licensed for your personal use only and may not be re-sold or given away. If you would like to share this publication with colleagues, family, friends, or students, please purchase an additional copy for each person (quantity discounts are available; contact us at info@hrcompliancetraining.Com for details).

Events, locations, characters, and people in this book are fictitious. Any similarity to actual events, places, characters, or people, living or dead is purely coincidental.

Written and produced in the United States of America.

Nothing to it but to do it
A Common Sense Guide to Your Dream Job

Davy Z Jones

"Ain't nothin' to it, but to do it." ~ Maya Angelou

Nothing to it but to do it

A Common Sense Guide to Your Dream Job

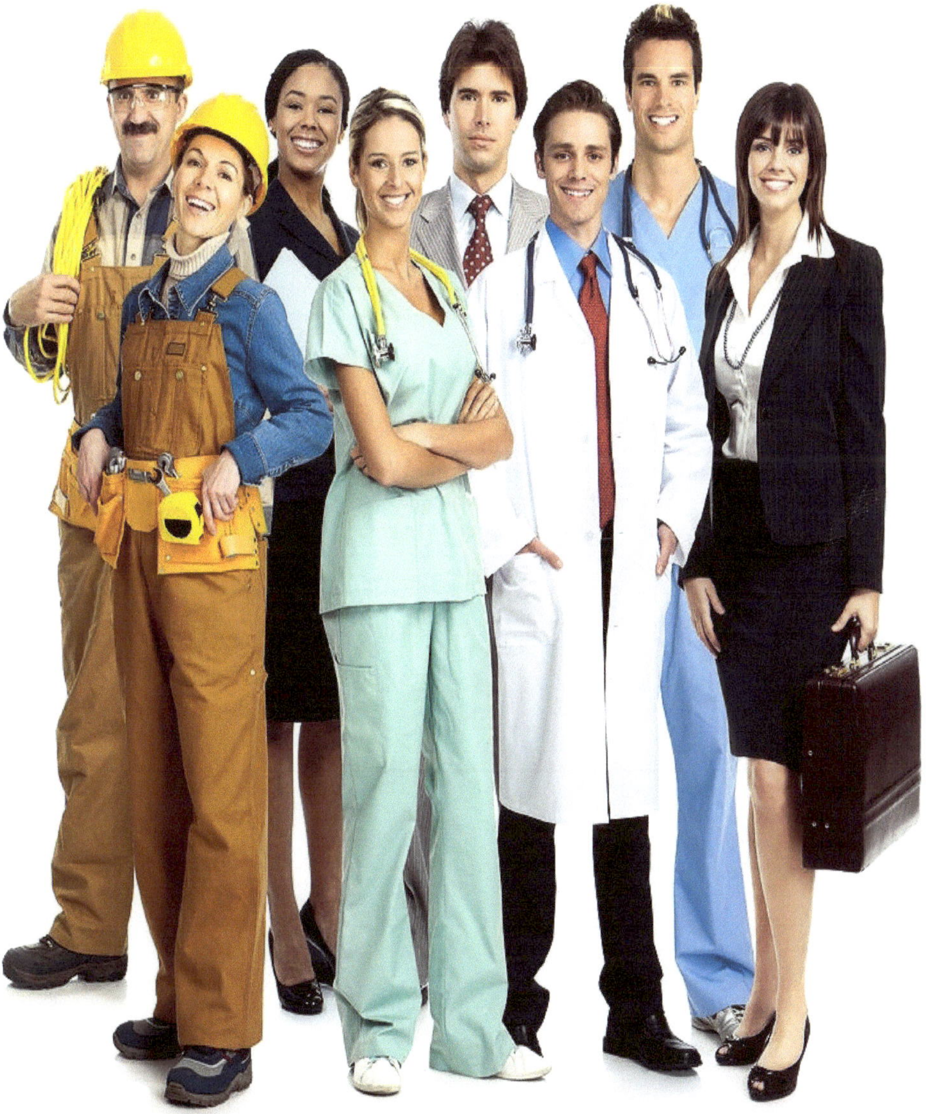

HRCT

Compliance for Success

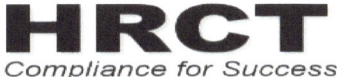

Nothing to it but to do it
A Common Sense Guide to Your Dream Job

© 2019 HRComplianceTraining.Com. All rights reserved.

Except as permitted under the U.S. Copyright Act of 1976, no part of this publication may be reproduced, distributed, or transmitted in any form or by any means, or stored in a database or retrieval system, without the prior written permission of the publisher.

Publisher:

HRComplianceTraining.Com

180 North University Avenue – Suite 270 – Provo, UT 84601

Author

Davy Z. Jones

First Edition: October 2019

ISBN -- 9781695197367

Nothing to it but to do it
A Common Sense Guide to Your Dream Job

Davy Z Jones

Contents

What is a dream job?	7
Common sense	10
You're not alone	12
Sometimes, a little inspiration is all you need	15
Chasing down a dream	19
Who you are, where you are, what you want to do	26
Who you are	27
Where you are	30
What you want to do	33
The resume and cover letter	37
Sample cover letter – experienced	45
Sample cover letter – inexperienced	46
Sample follow-up Email – resume and cover letter	48
The interview	51
Sample Email -- thank you for the interview	57
Sample Email -- if you decide to decline a job offer	59
Sample Email – if you decide to accept a job offer	61
You got the job -- now what?	62
Epilogue	65
References	67

*"Choose a job you love,
and you will never have to work a day in your life."*

~ Confucius

What is a dream job?

LET'S DEFINE A 'dream job' in simple, common-sense terms: *A dream job is doing what you love to do to support the lifestyle you've chosen.*

A dream job, however, is not a perfect job.

Far be it for a mere mortal like me to dare to disagree with essence of the

Confucius "never have to work a day in your life" quotation, but even if you have your dream job, you will have to 'work' at least a portion of just about every day.

Like any job, your dream job, will not allow you to do whatever you feel like doing all the time or any time, and will occasionally be annoying, demanding, tiring, and therefore not always so dreamy.

The moment you start your dream job, you'll naturally be excited, enthused, and anxious to prove yourself. But until you become acclimated, you won't know policies and procedures; you won't know who does what, why, where, and when, and you won't understand who has power and who doesn't.

You won't even know who you can trust, which means that an inadvertent misstep can turn your dream job into a nightmare.

So be patient and accept the fact that it will take time for you to settle into your dream job just as it will take time for your dream job to settle into you.

But so what?

You'll have what you've always wanted and, with time and patience, you'll ultimately overcome the uncertainties that typically frustrate any newbie.

So, let's get down to it.

What is your dream job, and where is it?

Not sure?

Let's go find out.

Nothing to it but to do it
A Common Sense Guide to Your Dream Job

Davy Z Jones

"Common sense is genius dressed in its working clothes."

~ Ralph Waldo Emerson

Common Sense

THIS BOOK WASN'T written by some supercilious egghead with more master's degrees and doctorates than "Carter has Little Liver Pills."

This book was written by me – someone who's worked at and enjoyed my dream job for the better part of my adult life.

I couldn't have completed this book if not for the ideas, suggestions, and tweaks offered by clients, colleagues, and friends – who, like me, are grateful to have relied on good old common sense to find and keep our dream jobs.

By the way, I should tell you that Merriam-Webster defines 'Common Sense' as: "*Sound and prudent judgment based on a simple perception of the situation or facts.*"

I like that definition. It's easy to understand and, like anything easy to understand, common sense is easy to follow.

Common sense isn't something you learn in a classroom or pick up from a book, not even this book. Like height, intelligence, or a pretty face, common sense is a gift you were born with, so, if you're one of the fortunate ones, be grateful.

Combine common sense with life experiences, and you'll be better able to make practical, reasonable, and ultimately reliable decisions about why, when, where, and how to find your 'dream job'.

An aside from the author: Forgive me for repeating myself so often in this book, but there is a method behind my madness.

You see, repetition is the easiest way to learn and remember. So, why not make learning and remembering as easy as I can?

Speaking of remembering, remember when you learned to ride your first bicycle? Remember when your mom or dad taught you how to drive? Remember when you learned to play tennis or pool? Your ability to stay up on two wheels, remain between the lines on the road, serve an ace, or sink the eight ball at the right time and in the right place, required repetition, known more commonly as practice.

Repetition works to help you learn and remember because it strengthens connections in the brain which increases your ability to apply everything you learn from this book so you can find and keep your dream job.

You're not alone

ACCORDING TO A 2017 study produced by Gallup titled "State of the American Workplace," nearly seventy percent of America's approximately 100 million full-time employees don't like their jobs.

Does that surprise you?

It shouldn't.

Since you're reading this book, it's reasonable to assume that you're one of  the approximately seventy million unhappy employees and, if so, you're obviously not alone.

You may be underappreciated, undervalued, and underpaid or you might not like how owners, managers, key personnel, and even colleagues take you for granted as if you're no more important than a bathroom fixture.

Or, you could be dissatisfied because your employer doesn't care enough to invest in fully training you to do the job you're expected to do.

Nevertheless, you can't forget that no matter where you work -- in a bodega, corporate office, delivery van, machine shop, medical facility, or in a warehouse -- it's your hard work along with the hard work of millions of your colleagues that generates the revenues and profits that keeps business going in America and around the world.

In light of that fact, you may be disillusioned and uncommitted, and you may tend to be late, fail to show up, or you might just walk away.

You may even be one of those glum employees who jump from job to job and never gets around to developing the skills you might have had if you'd managed to stay in a job for an extended period.

Even if you happen to be one of the lucky ones who's appreciated, respected, and well-trained, you may never be happy unless and until you settle into your 'dream job' where you are trusted to do what you do best with little interference and relatively few limits.

So, learn who you are, where you are, and what you want to do – and then go for your dream job so you can accomplish everything you ever wanted to achieve.

As Steve Jobs said, "The only way to do great work is to love what you do. If you haven't found it yet, keep looking. Don't settle."

It seems to me that Jobs was absolutely right.

Right?

"Don't compare yourself with anyone in this world; if you do so, you are insulting yourself."

~ William Henry Gates III

Nothing to it but to do it
A Common Sense Guide to Your Dream Job

Davy Z Jones

Sometimes, a little inspiration is all you need

SOUTHERN CALIFORNIA SKIES were bright, and the temperature was hovering near a hundred degrees as Mary Taylor drove north on Interstate 10 in air-conditioned comfort.

She was on her way home from a fun-filled 30th reunion weekend in Palm Springs and was happily reminiscing about Friday night football games, school dances, parties, prom dates, ditch day, and, of course, graduation day.

Mary had no way to know that her life about to be turned upside down and she'd finally have to put her fears aside and go after her dream job.

As traffic slowed, Mary glanced in the rearview mirror, caught her reflection, and wished she hadn't. At nearly fifty, with eye wrinkles deepening and jowls beginning to droop, the beauty that once attracted so much attention was fading fast, and she didn't like it – not one bit.

It was late afternoon when Mary turned on to her street in an Orange County gated community. She'd been yearning to see her husband after three long days away, but that feeling faded the moment she pulled into her driveway.

The garage door was open, and her husband's car was gone.

She turned off the engine and, not liking what she wasn't seeing, grabbed her phone, pressed speed dial 1, and waited until a recorded voice coldly said, "*The number you have dialed is no longer in service. Please check the number and try again."*

A pang of fear knifed through Mary, and she took a deep breath to rein in a deluge of alarming thoughts: *He should be home! Where's his car? Why is the garage door open? Why isn't his phone working? Where is he? Is he okay? Should I call 911?*

Beside herself with fear, Mary hopped out of her car and ran to the house and was surprised to find the front door unlocked. She went from room-to-room, anxiously calling for her husband, but he was nowhere around. Moreover, everything he valued – clothing, personal items, books, his computer, and golf clubs – was gone.

Stuck to a mirror in the master bathroom was a yellow post-it note on which her husband had scrawled five cryptic words: "I left to find myself."

At that moment, with a sickening feeling in the pit of her stomach, Mary faced a rotten reality: For better or for worse, she was on her own – the man with whom she shared her life for twenty-eight years would not be coming back.

To add insult to injury, Mary discovered the next day that her husband had drained their checking and savings accounts and canceled joint credit cards.

Mary worked as an assistant manager at a local bank where she earned enough to eke out a living for the immediate future, but she was going to have to find a much better paying job if she expected to keep the house and have enough money to rebuild her life.

What should I do? Should I grab the first better-paying job I can find? Or, at my age, should I try to get my dream job?

Mary's dream job was in sales but not in a retail store or a real estate office. As crazy as it may have sounded to others, Mary dreamed of selling heavy construction equipment.

In the summer between her junior and senior years at college, Mary worked as a receptionist at a construction equipment dealership where she developed a keen interest in how tractors worked and a curiosity about who bought them and why.

But that was then, and this was now, and, when it came to her dream job, Mary couldn't help but wonder, *who on earth would hire an inexperienced, middle-aged woman to sell construction equipment?*

Mary recalled something she heard years earlier in an English class. It was Ralph Waldo Emerson, a 19th Century poet, who wrote, *"What lies behind us and what lies before us are tiny matters compared to what lies within us."*

Emerson's words inspired Mary to put her fears aside and cold-call construction companies and equipment dealers to ask managers if they would be willing to let her interview them about their unique business concerns.

Persistence prevailed, and over time, Mary was able to convince half a dozen contractors and three sales managers to talk with her about their unique business concerns.

Mary prepared two lists of questions. One to prompt contractors to talk about what they expect from equipment dealers and one to ask sales managers to describe the attributes they look for in the ideal construction equipment sales representative.

After Mary completed the interviews and analyzed the information she gathered, she felt like she had a distinct advantage that just might convince an equipment dealer to hire her.

A month and a half after Mary's interview with sales manager Jay Flanagan, he called to tell her that he was looking to replace a sales rep who was retiring.

Flanagan was impressed with Mary's grasp of what contractors want when they purchase construction equipment and with her interest in what it takes to succeed as an equipment sales rep so he thought she might like to have a shot at the job.

Mary, of course, jumped at the opportunity and submitted a cover letter and resume and went through two interviews.

A week after the second interview, Flanagan called to offer Mary the job which included a comprehensive training program, a company car, an expense account, health insurance, profit-sharing, and a substantial salary.

Mary struggled to remain calm as she graciously accepted the position, and they agreed on a starting date.

Mary thanked Jay, and after she hung up the phone, she wiped the tears from her eyes, took a deep breath, and then gratefully recalled Emerson's inspiring words: *"What lies behind us and what lies before us are tiny matters compared to what lies within us."*

That was all the inspiration Mary needed -- *would it be enough for you?*

Chasing down a dream

IF YOU'RE CURRENTLY working, you've undoubtedly asked, why am I here? Do I feel valued, respected, and worthwhile, or is this job nothing more than a means of getting my hands on a potentially precarious paycheck?

Since you're reading this book, the answer to any or all aspects of that question is patently clear.

The critical question now is, *How would you feel if you could go to your dream job tomorrow morning and know that your efforts, ideas, and suggestions would make a difference not only in your life but in the lives of others as well?*

You'd feel great of course, and the way to get that dream job so you can feel those feelings is to:

Concentrate on getting happy

Focus on the interests, skills, and talents that give you a sense of fulfillment and satisfaction on the job. When you put your energies into focusing on what makes you feel happy and what gives you a sense of accomplishment and purpose, you'll be better able to define exactly what you're looking for in your dream job.

Go slow to go fast

Set aside time each day to chart your step-by-step approach to getting the dream job you deserve. If you're in school or working a full-time or part-time job, get up earlier and stay up later to research and evaluate jobs that closely align with your interests, skills, and talents.

Network, network, network and then network some more

More people get more jobs by word of mouth than they do from published sources – online or elsewhere.

So, tell everyone you know – friends, family, and the folks you do business with like your accountant, banker, barber, doctor, hairstylist, mechanic, and anyone else you know who might know someone somewhere who can introduce you to the right opportunity.

Don't hesitate to contact community organizations like the Chamber of Commerce and check out online sources like Careerbuilder.Com, Dice.Com, Facebook, Indeed.Com, and LinkedIn. Look into joining business networking groups. You'll be pleasantly surprised at how many of the good folks in those groups can not only identify with what you're trying to do but may be able to provide information that just might lead you to your dream job.

Talk, talk, talk, and then talk some more

Spreading the word is critically important, so find people who have your dream job or something close to it. Ask them what they're doing, why they're doing it, how they're doing it, and be sure to ask how they would make things better.

People love nothing more than to talk about themselves so, if, for example, your dream job is to become a nurse, find one, tell him what you're up to and invite him out to lunch or for coffee and ask for his advice.

I'd be surprised if he doesn't gladly tell you everything you want to know and more.

Read, read, read, and then read some more

With minimal effort, you can find loads of fantastic books on all aspects of career development and job hunting that can guide you from here to your dream job in less time and with greater ease than you might have imagined.

Check out References on page 67, and you'll see what I mean.

Do your research

Are you sure you know what it takes to get and keep your dream job? Do you know what abilities, interests, and skills you'll need to be a productive asset for a prospective employer or business partner?

Are you qualified to perform your dream job? If not, get the education you need at a community college, or a brick and mortar or online university.

By the way, if you can get a dream job internship that allows you to get real-time experience, seize the opportunity.

And, if you're middle-aged or beyond, don't fall for the 'you're past your prime' or the 'you're too old' malarkey. You are who you are, and chronology has nothing to do with your ability to perform well.

If that isn't true, can anyone explain how 70-year-old Benjamin Franklin managed to help draft the Declaration of Independence? Moreover, if age is such a limiting factor, how on earth did he continue to serve the nation well into his 80s?

Don't kid yourself

If your dream job is to become an airline pilot, and you're floating around the late-middle-age mark, you'll want to make it your business to learn something about mandatory retirement ages.

If your dream job is to become a teacher, but you don't have the education or experience to get your teaching credential, why not look for an opportunity to work as a teacher's aide or as a clerk in a school office?

You might discover that you can't put up with school district politics or the regimen. Or, you might find that your love for helping children learn is all the motivation you need to get educated so you can become the best teacher you can be.

Make sure that your dream job exists, that you will like it, and that you can live on whatever the pay might be. If the job isn't real or if you don't like it or if the compensation won't support the lifestyle you choose, don't hesitate to replace a probable nightmare with a potential new dream.

Don't chatter, do

Telling everyone or anyone about how you're going to find your dream job can become a substitute for actually doing it. It might feel good for a minute, but don't waste time trying to convince anyone, especially yourself, that you're finally going to do something meaningful with your life.

Stop talking and do the hard work – define your dream job, search for the right job with the right employer or business partner, prepare and submit individualized cover letters and resumes, and interview to win the right job for the right reasons.

Don't lock yourself into a rigid plan

There's no canned formula you can follow to get from here to your dream job so don't waste time, energy, and money trying to mimic a friend, relative, or idol no matter how similar your goals may seem to be. After all, your dream job is unique to you -- no one else has the desire, the insight, or the ability to create your pathway to success because only you can do what you can do.

Don't give up on you

Life ain't easy and life ain't always fun. So, it's understandable that when challenges pop up, you might fall into the trap of thinking that you don't have what it takes to convince a prospective employer or business partner to take a chance on you.

If you did fall into that trap and couldn't get out, you'd have to put this book down, forget about your dream job, and quit.

But you're not a quitter.

You know from your own life experience, and the lives of others – Vera Atkins, Winston Churchill, Henry Ford, Bill Gates, Steve Jobs, and Rosa Parks, -– all of whom failed before they finally succeeded, that the best way to guarantee success is to never quit.

If you could peek behind closed doors, you would likely see that most if not all of the great successes from all walks of life have the same conflicts, problems, self-doubts, and worries as do you and everyone else.

So, take a good look at yourself and give yourself a cheer for having the courage to take all the risks and do all the hard work required to pursue your dream job.

Trust the power implicit in your unique abilities, education, interests, skills, and talents and bet on yourself to find the wisdom and strength you'll need to get and keep the dream job you truly deserve.

Nothing to it but to do it
A Common Sense Guide to Your Dream Job

Davy Z Jones

"The future belongs to those who believe in the beauty of their dreams."

~ Eleanor Roosevelt

Who you are, where you are, what you want to do

ARISTOTLE, THE ANCIENT Greek philosopher and scientist who's often referred to as "The Father of Western Philosophy," left us with a memorable axiom when he said, "*Knowing yourself is the beginning of all wisdom.*"

How would you answer someone who asks, "Do you know who you are, where you are, and what you want to do?"

If you're not sure, you might want to find a quiet place where you can be alone and contemplate critical aspects of that rather complex three-part question.

You'll want to objectively think about where you came from, where you grew up, who raised you and how, where you went to school, who your friends were, what you did when you became an adult, when and how you've failed, and when and how you've succeeded.

Take your time, and be honest. Don't try to sugar-coat or glamorize your history to fulfill any unfulfilled fantasies. That'll only cloud your memory and prevent you from developing an accurate picture.

This exercise – *you will likely have to do it more than once* -- will help you determine where you're strong, where you're not so strong, and what you need to do to define, create, and find your dream job.

Who you are

THERE ARE 7.7 billion people in the world, and only one is you.

No one has your experience, your education, your ambitions, or thinks like you.

No matter who told you what you could or could not do and no matter who might say that you're not good enough to get your dream job, please know that they were, are, and will always be wrong.

Your abilities, dreams, education, experience, and talents are unique to you. So how on earth could any other person possibly know what you can or cannot do?

Moreover, since no one has the psychic powers it would take to define how good you are or could be, there is no reason to listen to anyone who in any way doubts your potential.

It's your life, and you can do anything you want to do -- provided you really want to do it.

That's an immutable truth, and you know it.

Don't you?

Of course you do, and you can't stop thinking: *I can do anything I want to do. I know it, and, deep down, so does everyone else, so why haven't I?*

The honest answer to that question may well lie in your willingness to give yourself some credit by acknowledging the following:

You don't have to talk, because you can do

You understand that there's no point in talking about what you want to do or even about what you 'plan' to do. You know that in order to get anywhere, you have to set realistic goals and you also have to invest whatever time and energy it takes to achieve those goals.

You know that you're good enough

When a critic puts you down, you don't believe them. You consider the source. If he or she never dared to find and keep his or her dream job, how can you trust anything they might say about you and your dream job?

You know what you want, and you know what you need

Needs always take priority over wants but needs often drive priorities. You think objectively about what you want, what you can have, and what you need to make sure your career goals are consistently realistic.

You know you well enough to be confident

While you aren't always right, you aren't usually wrong. Your confidence helps you set reasonable goals and enables you to work through to achieve the ultimate success you so richly deserve.

You never give up

Many talk about how they'd love to have their dream job but few are willing to do the hard work. You, on the other hand, are eager to work to get your dream job. And, if you fail, you use what you've learned to keep on keeping on because that is who you are.

You refuse to allow your inner critic to beat you down

You know very well that negative thinking is self-destructive. Negativity is your worse enemy because it will prevent you from creating and pursuing your dream job. You know that your ability to succeed depends in large part upon how you feel about you. So, you refuse to waste a moment of your valuable time beating yourself up.

You've learned to trust your inner voice

You know how important it is to separate fear-based negatives from fact-based positives that can pop up in your ongoing inner monologue. You believe your inner voice when it tells you that, if you have the desire and you're willing to work hard, you can overcome any challenge that might threaten your ability to get and keep your dream job.

Where you are

EVER FEEL LIKE you're immersed in the lives of others?

If so, that could be because you've spent a lifetime following the narrow path laid out for you by family, friends, colleagues, teachers, coaches, and social norms.

You know the route you're supposed to take: K-12 followed by a full-time job or a four-year university degree and maybe even graduate school or a professional certification. And then, after you've finished your education, whatever it may be, the path takes you to a job or profession you may not want or need.

That sound about right?

But, over the years, as you've matured and learned more about your interests and talents, you know that you're on the wrong path and you've come to appreciate the fact that you deserve your dream job.

At the same time, you may well have developed some real-world skills you'd like to put to work in your dream job.

It's important to remember that the primary reason you've decided to pursue your dream job, with all the inherent risks that come with that pursuit, it's because you're driven to perform and win.

You may be in sales, but your dream job could be in the cockpit of an airliner.

Nothing to it but to do it
A Common Sense Guide to Your Dream Job

Davy Z Jones

Or, you may be a food server, and your dream job could be on stage. Or, you might be a medical professional, and your dream job could be to serve with *Doctors Without Borders*. Or, you may be a CPA, and your dream job could be to research the effects of climate change. Or, you might be working in a car dealership, a grocery store, or a warehouse, and your dream job might be to become an attorney, a dentist, or a zookeeper.

Okay, at this point you might say, "Cut to the chase. How do I get out of the rat race I'm in and on to my dream job?"

Before anyone can answer that question, you have some work to do. You have to define, locate, and target that dream job, whatever and wherever it might be.

You have to ask and answer an intriguing question: *If I could wake up tomorrow morning and be able to do anything I want, what would I do?*

Now, if you've envisioned your dream job but you aren't entirely clear about how to match your abilities, education, interests, and skills to the job, you might want to try an online self-assessment tool.

While there are several excellent websites you can choose from; I suggest you start with a reasonably comprehensive site like The Muse.

If you'd like to have a fresh set of eyes evaluate who you are, where you are, and what you want to do, you might talk with a career counselor.

No matter which way you decide to go – on your own or with professional help – I guarantee one thing: You will enjoy the journey, and you will learn a lot about who you are, where you are, and what you want to do.

What you want to do

WHAT DO YOU want to do?

Think about what made you feel good at any point in time when you were working as an employee, an independent contractor, or as a volunteer? Were you doing something that would improve your life or the lives of others? Were you working alone, mentoring someone, or were you part of a team? Were you leading or were you following? Were you interacting with  people, or were you processing inanimate parts, pieces, or assemblies?

While relating what you enjoy doing to your dream job is a great way to define it, I'd like to say again that it would be helpful to contact some of the fortunate folks who are already doing what you think you'd like to do.

You'll want to ask them about what they like, what they don't like, and what they would change if they could.

If, for example, your dream job is in a classroom educating others, you ought to talk to teachers, school administrators, and parents.

If the health care profession is where you'll find joy and satisfaction, talk to EMTs, nurses, and doctors.

If your dream job is behind the wheel of a race car, get out to a race track and talk to drivers and crew chiefs. It might even be a good idea to attend a driving school so you can experience your dream job first hand.

The closer you get to your dream job, the more you'll know about whether or not to continue the pursuit.

A simple way to match you to your dream job

Since writing by hand expands thinking and sparks creativity, you might want to start by putting your mouse or your phone aside for a few minutes and get out a yellow pad and a pencil. List your interests and skills in column A.

Then, go back to your mouse or phone and do some online job searching.

You can go to any or all of the following job search sites like CareerBuilder, Glassdoor, IndeedJob, LinkedIn, Monster, RobertHalf, ZipRecruiter, or similar sites not listed here to start your search.

Most job sites give you the ability to search associations, company career sites, job boards, and other job postings.

Who knows? You may even find some new titles you hadn't considered.

Go back to your yellow pad, pick up your pencil, and, as you search, list the job titles that match your interests and skills in column B.

Cross-reference your interests and skills in column A to job openings in column B, and you'll know where to look for your dream job.

Doesn't sound too complicated, does it?

Research employers, online and in person, to learn everything you can about organizational culture, pay and benefits, upward mobility, and workplace environment.

After you've completed your job search research, evaluate the results, and narrow your list down to a manageable number of target employers.

Tailor your resume and cover letter to address the duties and responsibilities of each job posted at each target employer and be sure to emphasize how your unique skills, talents, and interests will improve productivity and increase profits.

Not every job opening is formally advertised or posted on a job board. So, if your target list isn't as comprehensive as you'd like, ask friends and family to let you know about possible dream job openings.

Attend conferences, career lectures, and industry seminars where you can let potential decision-makers know that you're hunting for your dream job.

You'll be glad you did.

> *"The secret of getting ahead is getting started."*
>
> ~ Mark Twain

The resume and cover letter

WITH NO MORE enthusiasm than you'd have for a root canal, it's time to face an ambitious challenge. In other words, it's time to showcase your experience, education, skills, and talents in a barely shameless effort to convince a recruiter, hiring manager, or potential business partner to risk their reputations and company money on you.

A well-written resume can create a positive first impression and can serve as a compelling introduction to who you are, where you are, and what you can do.

Most recruiters and hiring managers don't spend a whole lot of time reviewing a resume before deciding whether or not to call an applicant in for an interview so you'll want to be as concise yet as clear as you can be.

A one-page resume works well for someone who's applying for an entry-level job but if your dream job requires a specific educational background or unique skills, don't hesitate to include necessary details about education, experience, and your expertise in a two-page resume.

I wouldn't, however, recommend that you ever go beyond two pages.

Don't bother trying to sell yourself with fancy designs or graphics. You won't sway a prospective employer or business partner with vivid colors or wild shapes or even cool layouts. They only want facts.

If you plan to send your resume electronically, it is best to write it in Word and then send it as a secure PDF attachment. You only get one shot at submitting a resume, so you want to make sure the recruiter or hiring manager receives it just as you wrote it.

Write your resume in the first person. You aren't a narrator; you're speaking directly to someone who needs to get to know you. Make your words work for you, not against you, by writing plainly. I suggest using words and syntax that a sixth-grader would easily understand.

Organization is critical

The first third of your resume should include vital information your prospective employer or potential business partner will need to know. List your contact information, links to any professional network websites like Facebook or LinkedIn, and include a summary of your interests and qualifications, and most recent job(s) and educational information.

Don't go generic

The best way to communicate effectively with a prospective employer or business partner is to identify with their business, industry, or organization. If you're submitting your resume for a sales position, focus on your sales training and experience. List your qualifications in the same order as they were listed in the job posting.

Keep in mind that if you send a generic resume to multiple prospective employers, you risk getting caught up in an applicant tracking system programmed to search for keywords and qualifications which may well relegate you and your resume to perpetual anonymity.

Take advantage of a job scan website like The Muse, Resume Hack, or Word Cloud Generator, to increase your chances of putting your resume in front of the right people in the right places at the right time.

Shoot the moon

The recruiter, hiring manager, or prospective business partner who reviews your resume is interested only in what you can do. So, insert a skills section under contact information where you can list hard skills like accounting, computer programming, finance, language, mathematics, sales, web design, writing, and other quantifiable abilities.

Don't insult the resume reviewer's intelligence by overloading your skills section with fluff like your ability to file, type, or use software like Word. Additionally, don't bother trying to make yourself look good by including personality traits, no matter how appealing they may seem to you and others.

Last but not least, don't forget to include but do not overload this section with keywords.

Stuff you don't want to do in your resume

Your resume can make or break your chance to get your dream job, so don't include anything that doesn't very clearly make you a compelling candidate.

- Do not lie, exaggerate, or fudge anything in your resume – *EVER!*

- Don't bother with your mailing address. If a prospective employer is interested in contacting you, an Email address and phone number will do.

- Don't fail to spellcheck and proofread your resume word-by-word by reading it out loud as many times as is necessary to make sure you don't inadvertently shoot yourself in the proverbial foot.

- Don't feel compelled to include your entire career history. Employers want to know about your recent relevant educational achievements and work experience.

- Don't include awards, certifications, and special mentions unless they are directly related to the skills you need to perform your dream job.

- Don't include high school unless you have no trade school, community college, or four-year college experience.

- Don't include educational or work experience that occurred more than a decade ago unless that experience is essential to your main selling point.

- Don't reveal your age with graduation or work experience dates.

- Don't waste the resume reviewer's time by including references but do indicate that references are available on request. Anyone who wants to offer you a job will want to see some references, so be ready.

- Don't waste your time or the prospective employer's time by trying to impress with fancy words and irrelevant rhetoric. Simply stated, it won't work.

Get down to it

You go to the trouble of preparing and sending your resume for one reason and one reason only: To convince a prospective employer or business partner to hire you for your dream job and pay the salary justified by your education, experience, and skills.

So, help that prospective employer or business partner do just that by including important stuff like:

- Degrees, certifications, and professional licenses that prove you can productively perform your dream job.

- All forms of recent relevant work experience, including paid positions, internships, and volunteer jobs.

- Additional skills, including language fluencies or specific technical capabilities (pilot's license, etc.),

The cover letter

Do you really need to write a cover letter?

Perhaps the better question is, why not write a cover letter?

Since you're asking a hiring manager or recruiter to take a chance on you, someone who is virtually unknown and unproven, why not use a cover letter to paint a picture of who you are, where you are, and what you can do to increase productivity and profits?

In other words, why not give a prospective employer or potential business partner compelling reasons to bring you onboard?

What you should include in your cover letter

A cover letter (one page, no more) is how you reach a hiring manager, recruiter, or potential business partner to tell him or her why you're the best person for a specific job in their organization.

Talk briefly about what motivates you to want this job.

Relate your education, experience, skills, and talents to the job's duties and responsibilities and be sure to say that you understand and support the organization's mission statement (make it your business to know it).

Think of your cover letter as your 'elevator pitch' (so-called because you should be able to present it during a brief elevator ride) in which you tell a

prospective employer or business partner why your interests, credentials, and capabilities will make a positive impact on productivity and profitability.

If your research indicates that a prospective employer or business partner faces significant challenges, don't be afraid to suggest a viable solution. Your suggestion(s) will demonstrate that you understand the business and that you're a creative problem solver who is willing to take the initiative to recommend solutions to improve productivity and profitability.

If your experience is relatable to the duties and responsibilities of the job, be specific about your accomplishments without seeming to brag. For example, if you're dream job is in sales, you might say something like, "*I was assigned the poorest performing territory, and within twelve months, I increased annual sales from $2 million to $13 million, making it the best performing territory in the company.*"

If you want to become a sales professional but don't have hands-on experience, get some by interning. If you can't find an internship, take the initiative to survey a sales territory. The survey will allow you to identify customer needs and wants and measure the ability of a prospective employer to meet those needs and wants. If you want to 'wow' a hiring manager or recruiter, all you have to do is mention the survey in your cover letter.

It's important to remember that, since a relatively small percentage of applicants even bother to write a cover letter, your letter will undoubtedly help you stand out from your competitors.

What you shouldn't include in your cover letter

Your cover letter shouldn't rehash your resume; it should not include anything about your personal life, it should not include any mention of how much money you want or think you deserve, and, like your resume, it should not contain a lie, exaggeration, or fudge of any kind.

Don't include references. You've indicated in your resume that references are available on request and that will do.

Whether you're experienced or inexperienced, if you have questions about what you might want to say in your cover letters, you'll want to check out the following pages.

Sample cover letter – experienced

AJAX Engineering
Contact name and title
Street address
City, State, Zip

Date

Dear Jane Doe;

I am applying for the territory sales representative position, and I've enclosed my resume for your review.

I've thoroughly enjoyed working as a manufacturing representative and sales coordinator for ABC Engineering and am pleased to have been able to work with our team to increase sales over the past two years by sixty-three percent.

I am excited to have the opportunity to apply for this position because, with my education and experience, I will be able to hit the ground running to increase Ajax sales and profits.

I look forward to meeting with you to discuss how my qualifications will support your mission.

Regards,

Your name

Phone number:

Email address:

Sample cover letter – inexperienced

AJAX Engineering Date
Contact name and title
Street address
City, State, Zip

Dear Jane Doe;

I am applying for the territory sales representative position, and I've enclosed my resume for your review.

Without mentioning your company or its products and services, I just completed an independent survey of your sales territory and learned from current and prospective clients that there are several ways Ajax could increase sales and profits.

I very much appreciate having the opportunity to be considered for this position, and I look forward to discussing the results of my survey with you soon.

Regards,

Your name

Phone number:

Email address:

Send your cover letter and resume to each prospective employer or potential business partner via Email or the postal service.

A tip: If you're unable to send your cover letter and resume electronically, send them via Priority Mail. Your submission will arrive within a couple of days, you'll be able to track it, and it will be much more likely to be noticed.

Resume and cover letter follow-up

You can't expect a prospective employer to take time to acknowledge the receipt of your cover letter and resume much less keep you posted on the status of your application.

You can follow-up by sending a simple, to-the-point, Email to reaffirm your interest in the job and to let the prospective employer or potential business partner know that you've submitted a cover letter and resume.

Don't insult anyone's intelligence by sending a convoluted, wordy follow-up message he or she may not have the time or interest to read.

Include the job title and your name in the subject line and get to the point in the body of your Email. Say that you've applied for the position and that you're interested in having the job and then attach a copy of your cover letter and resume -- just in case.

Sample follow-up Email -- resume and cover letter

Subject line: Cloud Computing Engineer – Your name

Dear Jane Doe;

I submitted my resume and cover letter for the Cloud Computing Engineer position posted on roberthalf.com.

I want to take this opportunity to express my keen interest in interviewing for the job.

I've attached a copy of my cover letter and resume for your review and look forward to hearing from you at your earliest convenience.

Regards,

Your name

Phone number:

Email address:

No response to your follow-up Email?

Wait a week and resend your Email one time and one time only. If after another week, you don't hear anything, don't ruffle any feathers. Pass on this particular job, and move on.

The employer or potential business partner will remember you as someone who was not only cool but patient. Who knows? There may come a time when that memory prompts the employer or potential partner to pull up your cover letter and resume and give you a call.

After all, the second-best time to evaluate an applicant or a prospective partner is right after the first choice fails.

"One important key to success is self-confidence.
An important key to self-confidence is preparation."

~ Arthur Ashe

The interview

WHEN A PROSPECTIVE employer invites you in for an interview, find out who the interviewer will be. What's her name and background, and how long has she been with the organization? Is she in HR, or could she be the supervisor or department head who ultimately would hire you?

What about the organization? What does it do, and how does it produce and deliver products and services? Who are its customers or clients? Is it a start-up, or has it been in business for a while? Does the organization have a mission statement, and if so, what does it say, and are you prepared to tell the interviewer how you would support the mission statement?

Check out the organization's website to learn everything you can about its products, services, and market share.

And then, before your interview date, dress appropriately for the job you want, stroll into the company location where you'll have your interview and engage in a casual conversation with a receptionist. Tell him that you're scheduled to come in for a job interview and you'd like to get a feeling for how the company operates.

Once you get the conversation started, let the receptionist talk. He will very likely tell you more than you might have thought to ask.

If you can find a way to speak to more than one employee, do it. You want to dig as deeply as you can so you can get a clear sense of how employees interact with each other and with management.

If you can swing it, talk to customers or clients. Find out what they like and don't like about the organization and its products and services. Ask whether they think it would be a good place to work.

Face-to-face interactions with current employees and customers or clients will give you insights that can help you frame better answers and questions when you talk with your interviewer and will help you feel more at ease on interview day.

Be yourself

Don't try to con the interviewer into thinking you're something or someone you're not.

Be authentic – you are enough.

How you dress for the interview, how you carry yourself, and how you communicate will let the interviewer know that you're a thoughtful candidate who deserves thoughtful consideration.

Even if your cover letter is outstanding, and your resume confirms that you're the perfect person for the job, the interviewer will ask a series of questions devised to confirm that your interests, education, experience, personality, skills, and temperament line up with job requirements, with the organization's culture, and with your future goals.

Whenever possible, remind the interviewer how your education, experience, and skills will improve productivity and profitability.

The interviewer will ask a variety of questions designed to understand what is behind the claims you made in your cover letter and resume.

If, for example, the job requires you to be creative, the interviewer will ask

questions to confirm that you have a history of creativity along with a demonstrated ability to follow-through, to deliver on-time and on-budget. After all, creativity without deliverability is useless.

Since a job interview is a two-way street, you have a right and an obligation to make sure that the organization would be a good fit for you. So be prepared when the interviewer asks, "Do you have any questions for me?"

That could be the interviewer's way of letting you know that she may be about to tell you that she wants to schedule a second interview or introduce you to the final decision-maker or even offer you the job.

That question is more likely the final step the interviewer will take before she winds down the conversation so she can move on to the next applicant.

While you may not have a clue about what the interviewer has decided about your fitness for the job, you have as much at stake here as the employer does. So, take as much time as you need to ask open-ended questions about whatever is most important to you. If you fail to ask those questions and you do get hired, you may well look back on interview day in a few weeks and regret having taken a job you can't stand.

How much is too much?

Before you go in for the interview, research salary ranges for your dream job. If you can't find the right people to ask, you can go to a website like Glassdoor.Com or Indeed.Com or Payscale.com so you can be fully prepared to have the 'how much' discussion with the interviewer.

If the interviewer doesn't tell you about compensation but asks how much you expect to earn, talk about the salary you deserve based on your education, experience, demonstrated skills, and your ability to contribute to productivity and profits.

Be prepared to negotiate. Know in advance how much you would be willing to give, if necessary, to get your dream job. If you're not happy with

the interviewer's offer, be prepared to pursue an alternative.

If the salary isn't what you think you deserve, but you don't want to turn down the job, ask if there are incentive bonuses or commissions?

If you can't get what you feel like you deserve, don't settle for less by taking the job anyway -- you will ultimately regret it.

Be cool

It's just a job interview, not a life or death drama, and even though your dream job is essential to you for a lot of good reasons, it's not worth getting all nervous and upset. All that'll do is knock you off your game and probably out of contention.

So, be cool. Rely on your natural ability to relate honestly and respectfully to the interviewer who is, after all, just another human being who is probably no smarter and no better than you.

If you don't get the job, accept the experience for what it is. While you may never know for sure, you might not have gotten the job because the interviewer saw that it wasn't right for you. In any case, review your cover letter, resume, and the interview, and then figure out how to be better the next time so you can keep on keeping on until you do get your dream job.

No matter how you think the interview went, get the interviewer's business card so you can send a thank-you Email.

Don't try to sell yourself or get all flowery in that Email. Keep your thank you simple. Just write a few lines to express your appreciation and send it within 24 hours.

Points to Ponder

- You can gain some insight into what the prospective employer's workplace is like by how the interviewer conducts herself. If her questions are reasoned and calm, chances are the workplace is relatively stress-free. If, on the other hand, the interviewer is rigid and querulous, it is reasonable to assume that her persona may be reflective of the attitudes of managers, supervisors, and key personnel.

- Always treat prospective employers with dignity and respect in every communication; never push, never criticize, and never demand.

- Don't send multiple Emails or call more than once to follow-up because if you do, a prospective employer might get annoyed and drop you as a candidate.

No matter what happens, keep on keeping on.

Sample Email – thank you for the interview

You might try something like this:

Subject line: Systems Analyst – Your name

Dear Jane Doe;

Thank you for taking time out of your busy schedule to interview me yesterday for the Systems Analyst position.

I came away from our conversation reassured that it is indeed the dream job I've always wanted.

If there are any more questions I can answer or if there is any more information I can provide, please let me know.

I hope to hear from you soon.

Regards,

Your name

Phone number:

Email address:

When you get a job offer

If you've knocked it out of the park with your cover letter, resume, and interview, you won't be at all surprised to receive a job offer.

The chance to finally have your dream job may make you want to jump right in, accept the offer, and get to work.

However, you may not want to jump too far into the offer until you thoroughly understand what's involved with pre-employment background checks, physical tests, or other screenings. You also may want to understand salary, benefits, and any retirement plan before you say yes.

If you're not willing to accept the job, immediately contact the person who made the offer to say thank-you and to decline respectfully.

Be honest about your reasons but don't say anything critical. Last but not least, be sure to document your decision in an Email like the sample on the following page.

Sample Email -- if you decide to decline a job offer

Subject line: Design Analyst – Your name

Dear Jane Doe;

Thank you very much for the offer to join Ajax as a Design Analyst.

Ajax is a forward-looking firm with a bright future, but I will not be able to accept the position because it doesn't quite align with my career goals.

I sincerely appreciate your willingness to extend the job offer, and I wish you all the best in your efforts to match the right person to the Design Analyst position.

Regards,

Your name

Phone number:

Email address:

Assuming that you're happy with the conditions that come with the job offer and presuming that you're okay with the compensation package, it goes without saying that you should accept the offer and run with it.

Whether you accept a job offer over the phone or in person, document your acceptance, and express your appreciation in an Email before the end of the business day.

Do not forget to confirm details like compensation, job title, and start date.

You may want to take a look at the sample Email on the next page.

Sample Email -- if you decide to accept a job offer

Subject line: Design Analyst – Your name

Dear Jane Doe;

Thank you for your phone call today to offer me the Design Analyst job.

I gratefully accepted the position, and we agreed that my start date is August 7.

The compensation package you offered includes a base salary of $6,000.00 per month plus healthcare coverage and a 401k plan.

If there is any additional information you might need before August 7, please let me know.

I look forward to seeing you then.

Thank you again for this opportunity.

Regards,

Your name

Phone number:

Email address:

You got the job -- now what?

ALRIGHT – YOU GOT your dream job, and you're as happy as you can be.

And that's great because, after all you've done to get the job, you deserve to enjoy good feelings.

But, now what?

Well, you may not need to read any of this stuff, but I'll give it to you anyway. The choice to read or not to read is, of course, yours.

How to succeed on the job is not something you learn in any school, so let's take a few moments to review stuff you almost certainly already know.

Be the first to take on any challenge

Your employer or your business partner will be glad to know that he or she can count on you to be a team player; someone who stands up to take on any challenge anytime, anywhere. Take every opportunity to prove that you're willing to go beyond your job description to make the organization run more smoothly and more profitably than it did before you arrived.

Take the initiative whenever and wherever it's needed

Actively look for opportunities to find better ways to do your job and to improve procedures and processes.

Dare to be different to create value

Make sure your efforts result in the delivery of products and services, on-time and on-budget, if not sooner and for less. Don't be afraid to be different and to stand out from your colleagues.

I'm not advocating that you compete with others to curry favor from anyone; I'm saying that if you make yourself invaluable, you can help colleagues increase their value to the organization as well.

Never identify a problem without offering a solution

You will have problems – *even on your dream job* – and the key to being the best you can be is to head off any problem with a workable solution. While you might not always have an immediate solution for every problem, be on the lookout – try to anticipate problems, inform those who need to know, and offer solutions wherever and whenever possible.

Never complain, never explain

Business is not personal. Business is business. You're there to do everything you can to create and sustain a harmonious workplace while generating a return on your employer's or business partner's investment in you. Don't get involved in the fussing and complaining that often goes on in a workplace. Don't be afraid to ask questions or to challenge processes and procedures that may not work. And, never moan or groan about anything or anyone at work.

You are expendable

The truth is, everyone is expendable. That's why presidencies have four-year terms, and members of Congress are only guaranteed a two-year or six-year term. Like it or not, time has a way of catching up with everyone, even the best of us. Even great business leaders like Lee Iacocca had to retire. So, don't let your head get too big over your successes. Be humble, be grateful, and be mindful of the calendar.

Create your own professional growth plan

Don't wait around for the boss to come to you with a promotions calendar. It's your life, your income, and your dream job, so decide what you want out of the future, plan for it, and get it. It's in the best interests of your employer or business partner to get a solid return on their investment in you, so make sure to align your goals with the organization's goals.

Be flexible, accommodating, and easy on yourself and others

Look – we're all human beings. We're flawed; we get tired, we get sick, we get disappointed, and, unfortunately, we age. All of those things add up to one thing: we're not always going to be on the top of our games, we're going to make mistakes, and, some of us will fall by the wayside.

So, be the one person your colleagues and managers can count on to accommodate changing conditions; be the one who never loses sight of the bottom line, but more importantly, be the one who always remembers to put people first.

Epilogue

WHETHER YOUR DREAM job is to become a five-star chef, a firefighter, a rock star, or a teacher, the quest to get the job will be much different than doing it.

You've used your common sense to evaluate who you are, where you are, and what you want to do and, now, you're ready to start working at your dream job -- at last!

Congratulations. You did it.

You'll be working for a new employer or partner and though you'll want to jump right in and make a significant impact on your colleagues, managers, and, of course, the bottom line, it ain't gonna happen overnight.

You don't need me to tell you to give your new job your best effort. You'll do that and more, but I will remind you to pay particular attention to finding ways to improve productivity and add to the bottom line.

After all, those two things -- *productivity and profitability* -- will keep you in your dream job for as long as you want to be there.

At the same time, due to lack of experience, you may not be as fully prepared as you would like to be on day one. But, like most successful people, you'll use the challenges you face to improve your skills over time.

Trust the instincts that led you to pursue your dream job in the first place, and you'll consistently make the progress you need to climb the ladder from this dream job iteration to the next one.

Who could ask for anything more?

References

100 Conversations for Career Success: Learn to Network, Cold Call, and Tweet Your Way to Your Dream Job – by Laura M. Labovich and Miriam Salpeter

A Matter of Difference – by B. M. Ferdman and M. N. Davidson

Common Sense – by Thomas Paine

Creating and Sustaining Diversity and Inclusion in Organizations: Strategies and Approaches -- by E. Holvino, B. M. Ferdman, and D. Merrill-Sands

Do What You Are: Discover the Perfect Career for You Through the Secrets of Personality Type -- **by** Paul D. Tieger and Barbara Barron-Tieger

Give Yourself a Raise -- **by** Gordon Bennett

How to Find Fulfilling Work -- by Roman Krznaric

Knock 'em Dead: The Ultimate Job Search Guide -- by Martin Yate, CPC

Leave Your Mark: Land Your Dream Job. Kill It in Your Career. Rock Social Media – **by** Aliza Licht

Life Reimagined: Discover Your New Life Possibilities -- by Richard J. Leider and Alan M. Webber

The 20-Minute Networking Meeting: How Little Meetings Can Lead to Your Next Big Job -- by Marcia Ballinger and Nathan A. Perez

The Inclusion Breakthrough -- by F. A. Miller & J. H. Katz

The Pathfinder: How to Choose or Change Your Career for a Lifetime of Satisfaction and Success -- by Nicholas Lore

The Power of Inclusion -- by M. C. Hyter and J. L. Turnock

What Color is Your Parachute? A Practical Manual for Job-Hunters and Career-Changers -- by Richard N. Bolles

What is Common Sense -- by Professor John McCarthy

You Deserve to Love Your Job: 20 Big Ideas for Succeeding in the New World of Work Kindle Edition -- **by** Alexis Grant

Nothing to it but to do it
A Common Sense Guide to Your Dream Job

Davy Z Jones

If you have any questions or comments, please contact us at 877-763-2752 or send an Email to davy@hrcompliancetraining.com

HRComplianceTraining.Com

180 North University Avenue – Suite 270 – Provo, UT 84601
Phone: 877-763-2752 – Email: info@hrcompliancetraining.Com
© 2019 HRComplianceTraining.Com. All rights reserved.